10 MINUTE MOMENTS

smart stuff

EXPLORING
PROVERBS
10 MINUTES
AT A TIME

simply for students

KURT
JOHNSTON

10-Minute Moments: Smart Stuff
Exploring Proverbs 10 Minutes At a Time

Copyright © 2009 Kurt Johnston
Visit our website: simplyyouthministry.com

All rights reserved. No part of this book may be reproduced in any manner
whatsoever without prior written permission from the publisher, except where
noted in the text and in the case of brief quotations embodied in critical articles
and reviews. For information, e-mail Permissions at inforights@group.com, or write
Permissions, Group Publishing, Inc., P.O. Box 481, Loveland, CO 80539.

ISBN: 978-0-7644-4137-0

Credits
Authors: Kurt Johnston
Executive Developer: Nadim Najm
Chief Creative Officer: Joani Schultz
Assistant Editor: Rob Cunningham
Cover Art Director: Veronica Lucas
Designer: Veronica Lucas / Daniel Sanchez
Production Manager: DeAnne Lear

Unless otherwise indicated, all Scripture quotations are taken from the Holy Bible,
New Living Translation, copyright © 1996, 2004, 2007. Used by permission of
Tyndale House Publishers, Inc., Carol Stream, Illinois 60188. All rights reserved.

10 9 8 7 6 5 4 3 2   17 16 15 14 13 12 11 10
Printed in the United States of America.

INTRODUCTION

Hey!

I probably don't know you, but I am proud of you. The fact that you are reading this little book means that you are interested in spending a few minutes with God every day. Be warned—even 10 minutes a day reading the Bible and talking to God will have a radical effect on your life! And because you are open to that idea, I am proud of you.

I like fortune cookies—I like them a lot! Now to clarify, I don't like the way fortune cookies taste (how could anybody like the way they taste unless you like the taste of cardboard). I like what's inside fortune cookies. Every single fortune cookie contains a wonderful little word of wisdom or prediction of the future—some sort of "fortune" for the person lucky enough to crack open the cookie!

Can I tell you a secret? Even though I like reading the fortunes, I know they usually aren't true—I certainly don't believe some dude in a cookie factory knows my future! The truth is, the main reason I like fortune cookies is because it's fun to add "at my grandma's house" at the end of each fortune: "You will find riches and fame sometime soon...at my grandma's house." "The wise person speaks slowly...at my grandma's house!"

What if I were to tell you that there is a book in the Bible that is made up almost entirely of short, interesting, and 100 percent true words of wisdom? Well guess what? The book of Proverbs is like a collection of God's fortune cookies—without having to eat cardboard!

In Smart Stuff, my friend Josh Pease and I picked 30 verses from the book of Proverbs that we think will challenge you, stretch your faith, encourage you, and make you a little smarter as you try to live a life that pleases God. Our hope is that by spending 10 minutes each day reading a proverb, reflecting on it, and talking to God about it, you will learn more about his ways and grow in your relationship with him.

Each proverb is God's voice speaking directly to you. (How awesome is that!) I hope you will let God's truth speak to you as you read each little chapter of Smart Stuff. And by the way, feel free to add "at my grandma's house" after each one if you want, because God's Word is true everywhere—even at your grandma's house!

Praying for you,

Kurt Johnston

Day 1

GOD: THE ULTIMATE GPS SYSTEM!

In my opinion, one of the best inventions in the history of humanity (other than donuts) are those GPS directional things that help you find your way around. I'm talking about the ones with the little voice that talks to you and tells you exactly when to make each turn. I'm pretty bad at finding my way around, so those things are great. Wouldn't it be awesome if life were like that? Imagine if we had someone giving us perfect advice for almost every decision we face. How awesome would that be? Well, believe it or not, that is exactly how God sees himself, and he wants us to see him that way, too!

Check out this first verse as we start our 30-day journey through the book of Proverbs.

2 MINUTES

Trust in the Lord with all your heart; do not depend on your own understanding. Seek his will in all you do, and he will show you which path to take (Proverbs 3:5-6).

5 MINUTES

- What do you think it means to trust someone with "all your heart?" Have you ever trusted someone that much? What does it mean to trust God that way?
- What do you think it means to "not depend on your own understanding"?

- Notice that it doesn't say, "seek God's will with whatever's bothering you" OR "with whatever you want." How does this verse encourage us to seek God's will? What does it say will happen if we do that?
- What is one area of your life where you don't trust God or where you know you aren't following God's plan? How could you work on that this week?

Hanging out with God

Spend a few minutes talking to God about what you just learned. If you need to, use the ideas below to get started:

- If there are things in your life that you know don't make God happy, tell him about those areas. Ask for God's help in living the way he wants you to live.
- If you're going through something tough and you don't know what to do, or you're facing a situation that seems really overwhelming, spend a few minutes talking to God about that. Ask him to give you directions during the day on how to deal with this situation.

This space is here for you to jot down some thoughts, write out a prayer, draw a picture, or do whatever you want to help you remember your 10-minute moment.

Day 2

JUST WHEN I THOUGHT I WAS GETTING AWAY WITH IT

I'm not proud of this, but when I was in junior high I went through a little season of doing all kinds of stuff that I knew I shouldn't do—stuff that would get me in tons of trouble if I ever got caught. But the reality is, I never got caught! At the time, I thought I was getting away with stuff so I just kept right on doing it. But eventually I learned that just because I had never technically been "caught" didn't mean I was getting away with it either. My behavior was causing all kinds of problems for me and my friends. Because I had never read today's verse, I had no idea that God's wisdom and truth were being played out in my life!

2 MINUTES

An evil man is held captive by his own sins; they are ropes that catch and hold him (Proverbs 5:22).

5 MINUTES

- Has there ever been a time in the past when you got caught doing something wrong? What was the punishment?
- Just because you get away with something (don't get caught) do you think there is a different kind of consequence? What are the consequences for a kid who DOESN'T get caught?
- What's one thing in your life that you know isn't what God wants for you? Why do you think it doesn't make God happy? What are some of the consequences he wants to protect you from?

3 MINUTES

Hanging out with God

Spend a few minutes talking to God about what you just learned. If you need to, use the ideas below to get started:

- The Bible says that God's power working through us is greater than any temptation or bad habit. Is there an area of your life that comes to mind? Ask God for his help.
- Usually part of the way God helps us get out from bad choices is through the help of other people. Ask God to show you one person who could help you—one person you could talk to about the area where you're struggling.
- Remember that no matter what you've done, God unconditionally loves you. Thank him for always being with you no matter what.

THOUGHTS

This space is here for you to jot down some thoughts, write out a prayer, draw a picture, or do whatever you want to help you remember your 10-minute moment.

Day 3

THIS VERSE BUGS ME!

I'm not really a "bug" guy. I prefer to avoid most of them. Spiders kind of creep me out. Roaches are my archenemy. I HATE roaches! In fact, just typing the word "roach" makes me squirm. But according to the Bible bugs aren't all bad. Today's passage even says we can learn a thing or two from them—not from roaches, though. They're evil.

2 MINUTES

Take a lesson from the ants, you lazybones. Learn from their ways and become wise! Though they have no prince or governor or ruler to make them work, they labor hard all summer, gathering food for the winter. But you, lazybones, how long will you sleep? When will you wake up? A little extra sleep, a little more slumber, a little folding of the hands to rest—then poverty will pounce on you like a bandit; scarcity will attack you like an armed robber (Proverbs 6:6-11).

5 MINUTES

- According to this passage, what can you learn from observing ants?
- Did you know before now that the Bible actually uses the word "lazybones"? Twice in this passage alone! Why do you think God gets so frustrated with lazy people?
- This verse talks about how ants don't have some boss making them work. Are you good about getting stuff done on your own, or do you always need a parent or teacher putting pressure on you?
- On a scale of 1-10, how much do you struggle with being lazy?

5

- The truth is that God has created each of us to do GREAT things. Every person has been given gifts and abilities to make our mark on the world around us. And when we're lazy we WASTE those gifts! That's why it's such a big deal to God.

Hanging out with God
Spend a few minutes talking to God about what you just learned. If you need to, use the idea below to get started:

- If there's an area of your life where you know you could be working harder, ask God to help you see that area of your life like HE sees it. Ask God to give you the motivation today to do your best.

This space is here for you to jot down some thoughts, write out a prayer, draw a picture, or do whatever you want to help you remember your 10-minute moment.

BURIED DEEP

Have you ever noticed how it's easy to memorize some things, but really hard to memorize others? For instance, I can still remember all the words to songs I learned in second grade, but I can't remember the names of people I met yesterday. In fact just yesterday I looked at my son and said, "Who are you?" OK, that's not true, but at my age it's probably gonna happen any day now!

I hate to admit this, but for me memorizing Bible verses usually falls into that second category of "hard to do." But it doesn't have to be. And because it's so important, I'm working on ways to get better at it.

2 MINUTES

Follow my advice, my son; always treasure my commands. Obey my commands and live! Guard my instructions as you guard your own eyes. Tie them on your fingers as a reminder. Write them deep within your heart (Proverbs 7:1-3).

5 MINUTES

- According to this verse, why is it important to obey God's commands? (The answer is right before the exclamation mark.)
- According to this verse, what are a couple ways to always remember God's commands?
- Since you probably won't tie Bible verses to your fingers, what is another way or two that might help you remember more of God's Word?

- What do you think it means to write something "deep within your heart?"

Hanging out with God

Basically, these verses are saying to surround yourself with God's commands where you can always see them (write them on your finger) and then memorize them and live them out so that they become a part of who you are (write them within your heart). Now, I know memorizing sounds a) boring and b) well, boring. So start with an easy one! Try this verse that we talked about a couple days ago: *Trust in the Lord with all your heart; do not depend on your own understanding (Proverbs 3:5).*

That's it—just two sentences! Now write this verse down on a note card or a spare piece of paper. Figure out a way that you can carry it around with you today so that you'll see it, and when you do just repeat it to yourself a couple times. Try to eventually do it without looking. And after you read it just say a short prayer to God— something like, "God, help me to trust you today. Help me to believe YOUR way is better."

As a matter of fact, instead of having some prayer thoughts right now, make the process of memorizing this verse your prayer to God today. And by tomorrow you can have a new verse buried deep in your heart!

This space is here for you to jot down some thoughts, write out a prayer, draw a picture, or do whatever you want to help you remember your 10-minute moment.

Day 5

ALL YOU NEED IS LOVE

I'm sure you've noticed that there's a lot of fighting in the world. As I write this, the United States is currently fighting people in two different countries. There are reports of fighting and deaths within other countries in the Middle East and South America. Countries like North Korea are building massive weapons that could instantly wipe out millions. This is nothing new—history is marked by countries being in conflict.

But there's also fighting on a much smaller scale. There's conflict between different groups at school—maybe between people of different races or ideas, or even conflict between people who just dress differently. There's conflict between friends. Between enemies. Between families. There's even conflict between my son's comb and his hair! There's LOTS of fighting around. What can we DO about all of that?

2 MINUTES

Hatred stirs up quarrels, but love makes up for all offenses (Proverbs 10:12).

5 MINUTES

- According to this verse what causes fighting?
- What makes up for all offenses?
- What do you think love is—is it mostly a feeling or a choice? How do you put it into action?

- Who are some people in your life that you're experiencing conflict with? How did things get to this place? What could you do to make it better?

The reason most conflicts don't go away is because we're convinced the other side is wrong and owes us something. We feel disrespected or hurt or cheated, so we treat other people poorly—we fight, lie, cheat, gossip, or steal right back—to "get even." But getting even never works—as a matter of fact it usually only makes things worse. What this verse says is that to make conflicts go away you have to stop making things all about you, and start choosing to love other people by forgiving them. I know—it's way easier said than done, but it's worth aiming for.

Hanging out with God
You can start today. If there's someone in your life you need to forgive, then start by talking to God—use the rest of this space to write a quick note to God, asking him to help you forgive the person you're struggling to love.

This space is here for you to jot down some thoughts, write out a prayer, draw a picture, or do whatever you want to help you remember your 10-minute moment.

Day 6

GOSSIP GIRL:
THIS GOES FOR GUYS, TOO

Let's be honest about this—it's really fun to be the first to know something. I love giving people the scoop on something they know nothing about. Sometimes this is harmless—like being the first to see the new blockbuster movie and telling all your friends about it the next day. But sometimes there's a really dark side to this...

2 MINUTES

A gossip goes around telling secrets, but those who are trustworthy can keep a confidence (Proverbs 11:13).

A gossip goes around telling secrets, so don't hang around with chatterers (Proverbs 20:19).

5 MINUTES

- Do you know people who are famous (in a bad way) for being gossips? What kind of reputation do they have?
- Have you ever spread a rumor about someone, knowing it would hurt that person? What made you decide to do that?
- Why do you think gossiping can be so fun? Why is NOT gossiping so hard?
- How does the second verse say to avoid gossip?

The truth is that it's SO easy to get sucked into the gossip game. People are talking bad about someone, and the next thing you know, you are, too. Or maybe YOU'RE the person deliberately spreading rumors about other people.

Whatever role you play in gossiping, the Bible is clear that we're supposed to be the kind of people who can be trusted—that we won't go around sharing stuff with people they don't need to know! If somebody shares something with us, we should be trusted to keep it to ourselves. (Of course, some secrets shouldn't be kept—like the kind that could lead to somebody getting hurt or doing something dangerous.)

Hanging out with God
Spend some time praying today about gossiping:
- If you are currently caught in a pattern of gossiping, ask God to help you change.
- Pray for the courage to not talk about other people, even when everyone else is doing it.
- Ask God to help you have HIS perspective on the people who are the targets of gossip.
- Ask that God would make you the kind of person known as trustworthy and kind.

This space is here for you to jot down some thoughts, write out a prayer, draw a picture, or do whatever you want to help you remember your 10-minute moment.

Day 7

MONEY
MONEY
MONEY

Have you ever heard the saying, "money makes the world go 'round"? I'm no scientist, but I think there are some other factors in the universe that actually cause the world to spin around! But I would agree that sometimes it seems as if this world revolves around money—it sure seems to be a big part of what we all focus on. And to some degree it makes sense. We need money to buy food, we need money to buy clothes, we need money to download songs, we need money to go to the movies, we need money to pay our friends (wait, am I the only one who has to pay my friends to hang out with me?), and the list goes on and on. It's no wonder so many people are so stressed out when it comes to money. In today's verse God warns us about putting too much trust in money or letting it become too important.

2 MINUTES

Trust in your money and down you go! But the godly flourish like leaves in spring (Proverbs 11:28).

5 MINUTES

- What does the first half of this verse mean?
- The second half of this verse says "the godly flourish." What do you think that means?
- If trusting in money gets people in trouble, what are godly people trusting in?
- If tomorrow you had to give up every possession that you own, what would be the hardest thing to get rid of, and why?

God doesn't want us to get caught in the trap of trusting in STUFF to make us happy, because ultimately stuff will always let us down. Stuff breaks. It gets old, outdated, and boring. Think about Christmas when you were 5 years old. Can you even remember what toy you wanted more than anything else? If you were lucky enough to find it under your Christmas tree, do you still have it? Probably not.

Hanging out with God

Do you have some "stuff" that you're a little too attached to? What would it be like to give it up for one week? If there's something that comes to mind for you, write it in the space below. Then write one or two sentences about your plan to give it up for the week. After that, say a short prayer to God, asking him to help you focus on him instead of stuff. Remember, we're doing all of this so that we can learn to lean on God and discover how much he loves us!

This space is here for you to jot down some thoughts, write out a prayer, draw a picture, or do whatever you want to help you remember your 10-minute moment.

Day 8

WHAT TO DO WHEN SOMEONE INSULTS YOUR MOM (SORTA)

OK, today's moment doesn't really have anything to do with your mom being insulted, but it DOES have to do with dealing with insults.

I don't know about you, but I don't handle being insulted very well. If I feel like someone is talking down to me, or making fun of me, or not giving me the respect I think I deserve, I tend to get angry—but according to today's verse, that's not how people who love God are supposed to respond.

2 MINUTES

A fool is quick-tempered, but a wise person stays calm when insulted (Proverbs 12:16).

5 MINUTES

- What does it mean to be quick-tempered? How would you describe that in your own words?
- According to this verse, what does a wise person do when insulted? Why does a wise person respond that way?
- Think back to a time when someone made fun of you, or criticized you, or a time you felt disrespected. How did you react—and why did you react that way?
- Why is it so hard not to lash out at others when they insult us? Why do we usually feel the need to "get even?"

If we're honest with ourselves, the reason it's so hard to be calm when we're insulted is because what other people think of us REALLY IS important to us! We don't like to admit that sometimes, but it's true. But the cool thing about being a child of God is that our value comes from the fact that God loves us, not from what other people think. The more you and I can accept that love, the less we will worry about what other people think.

Hanging out with God
In the space below, write a short paragraph prayer to God. Maybe you'll want to focus on not being angry at other people. Or maybe you'll want to ask God to help you know his love better. Or maybe you'll just want to thank God for how much he loves you. Whatever you do, go through today remembering that because of how much God loves you, you don't have to worry so much about what other people think.

Oh, and don't even think about insulting my mom! Oops...maybe I need to reread what I just wrote.

This space is here for you to jot down some thoughts, write out a prayer, draw a picture, or do whatever you want to help you remember your 10-minute moment.

Day 9

BE HEALED

If you've ever read the book (or seen the movie) *The Lion, the Witch, and the Wardrobe* (part of a series of books known as *The Chronicles of Narnia*) then you'll remember that little Lucy, the youngest of the children, was given a very special gift by Aslan the Lion—the power to heal. Using a little vial full of a magical liquid, Lucy was able to heal the deepest of wounds.

How awesome would that be, if you could go up to someone who just wiped out on a skateboard, throw some water on them, and magically all the scrapes would go away! Well, today's verse says that we actually DO have the power to heal. It might not be outside wounds (that's what Band-Aids are for), but we DO have the power to heal wounds people have in their hearts.

2 MINUTES

Some people make cutting remarks, but the words of the wise bring healing (Proverbs 12:18).

5 MINUTES

- What does it mean to "make cutting remarks?" What's another way of saying that?
- How can "the words of the wise bring healing?" What do you think that means?
- Can you remember a time when someone said something that made you feel great? What did that person say? Why did it feel so good?

17

- Think about your own life. Do you tend to say more words that cut down or words that heal?

The truth is that your words have a LOT of power. You can tear people down or build them up. You can make them feel like less of a person, or you can make them feel valued and loved.

Hanging out with God

So how can you today use your words to build up and heal people instead of tearing down and hurting people? Spend some time praying that God would help you become someone who uses kind words, then make a list of people you can think of who need "healing" through your words. Maybe it's someone you said something mean to recently, and you need to apologize to that person. Maybe it's just someone who could use an encouraging note, or maybe you can think of something kind to say to somebody who gets teased a lot. Before you're done today write down the name of one person who could use some kind words. Then pray that God would use your words to bring some healing.

This space is here for you to jot down some thoughts, write out a prayer, draw a picture, or do whatever you want to help you remember your 10-minute moment.

Day 10

KURT THE RUBBER KNIFE THIEF

In my entire life, I have only stolen one thing. I was 5, and my neighbor had a really cool collection of rubber knives. Looking back on it, I'm not sure why a 5-year-old kid would have a rubber knife collection, but my buddy did. He had lots of rubber knives; certainly he wouldn't miss one, would he? So one day when he wasn't looking I grabbed the biggest, baddest rubber knife in his collection and snuck it out of his house.

Sadly, I didn't have much time to enjoy it. As soon as I set it on my nightstand to admire it, I was overwhelmed with guilt. How could I take something that wasn't mine? What would my mom and dad say when they found out? Why would I do something like this to my friend? Is Jesus going to zap me with lightning when I go to sleep tonight?

Guilt is an interesting thing. It can be bad if it causes you to dwell on the past or to not forgive yourself. But it can also be really, really good. Look at today's verse:

2 MINUTES

Fools make fun of guilt, but the godly acknowledge it and seek reconciliation (Proverbs 14:9).

5 MINUTES

- What does it mean to "acknowledge" something?

- Why do you think it says that godly people acknowledge guilt? What does that mean?

Basically, this verse says there are two responses to feeling guilty: making fun of it or responding to it. The truth is that sometimes guilt is a good thing. If you rob a bank or hit your sister, then feeling guilty is the right reaction. If you rob a bank then go home and hit your sister, then you should really feel guilty! And the right way to respond to guilt is to make things right: Give back the money and apologize to your sister (that's what reconciliation means—to make something right).

- Have you ever felt bad about something you did that was wrong, but then someone else told you "it's no big deal?" What does this verse say about that?
- When we do something wrong, who is the main person we need to make things right (reconcile) with?

Hanging out with God

Guilt can be a good thing because it moves us to make things right with God. HE is the first person we always have to make things right with. And what's cool about God is that he doesn't stay mad at us—the Bible says that the moment we confess what we've done, God wipes it away and doesn't remember it anymore. It even says that for those of us who have decided to follow Jesus, he has already forgiven everything—we just have to admit to what we did and accept God's immediate forgiveness!

- Is there something you've done that is making you feel guilty? How can you make that right with God? Spend some time praying to him about this.
- Is there something in life that you did a long time ago, and have already made right, but STILL feel guilty about? If so then talk to God about that, and know that he DOESN'T want for you to beat yourself up over the past. Ask him to help you know you're forgiven.

THOUGHTS

This space is here for you to jot down some thoughts, write out a prayer, draw a picture, or do whatever you want to help you remember your 10-minute moment.

Day 11

ADVICE YOU CAN TRUST

I have a friend who believes just about everything she hears—especially if it's from somebody she knows or somebody who is labeled as an "expert." I could tell her that a three-legged polar bear was just discovered in Kenya riding a unicycle and her response would probably be, "Cool—what color was the unicycle?" She is one of the most trusting people I know—and one of the easiest to trick! Being trusting is a good quality to have. But at the same time, we shouldn't trust everyone all of the time, right? Because sometimes being too quick to believe everything we're told can lead to problems. Today's verse warns us not to believe everything we hear.

2 MINUTES

Only simpletons believe everything they're told! The prudent carefully consider their steps (Proverbs 14:15).

5 MINUTES

- A "simpleton" is a way of describing someone who doesn't think things through very well. What are some words you might use to describe that kind of person?
- Being "prudent" is a way of describing someone who DOES think things through before acting. What are some words you'd use to describe THIS kind of person?
- There are lots of people who are telling you things—can you think of some that maybe you shouldn't trust?

- This verse says "the prudent carefully consider their steps." What do you think it means to "consider your steps"? What's another way of saying that?
- Are you the kind of person who tends to think things through before you act, or do you tend to make decisions without thinking?
- What are some of the dangers of thinking things through too much?
- What are some of the dangers of not thinking things through enough?

Hanging out with God

God doesn't want us to be the kind of people who listen to bad advice and make harmful choices. Spend some time praying to God today about making good choices. Ask him to give you wisdom to know which people you should listen to, what to believe, and what you should do.

This space is here for you to jot down some thoughts, write out a prayer, draw a picture, or do whatever you want to help you remember your 10-minute moment.

Day 12

EAT YOUR VEGETABLES

His name was Tony, and he was the class bully. Sometimes he would be nice to me; sometimes he wouldn't. But I remember that I DESPERATELY wanted to be friends with Tony—not just so the bullying would stop, but so I could be popular like him. I thought if he and I were friends, people would accept me. I was willing to be friends with someone I didn't like, just so I could get something out of it. That's what today's verse is about.

2 MINUTES

A bowl of vegetables with someone you love is better than steak with someone you hate (Proverbs 15:17).

5 MINUTES

- Forget whether or not you prefer vegetables or steak. Here's the point of this verse: It's better to be poor and with people we love, than rich and with people we hate. Do you agree or disagree? Would you be OK being poor if you were with people you loved? Why or why not?
- Have you ever chosen to hang out with people you didn't really like so you could get something? How happy were you during that time?

The verse isn't really talking about the people we're hanging out with—it's talking about our priorities. Have you ever seen adults in jobs they hate, but they stick around only for the money? It happens all the time. Sometimes specific people marry for popularity, or for money, or for social status, even though they don't really love the other person.

- Why do you think people do this?
- Is there anything in your life that's interfering with your really good friendships? How can you make a change to help balance that out?

Today's verse is a super practical one—it's basically just saying "don't let stuff become more important than people."

- Is there any area of your life where "stuff" has become more important than "people"? If so, draw a picture of it in the space below.

Hanging out with God
Spend some time asking God to help you love people more today. Maybe you should ask him to help you like veggies a little more, too!

This space is here for you to jot down some thoughts, write out a prayer, draw a picture, or do whatever you want to help you remember your 10-minute moment.

Day 13   STUBBORN

I kind of have this problem: I always want to do things MY way. Whenever someone tells me I can't do something, I immediately want to do it. If someone tells me my way isn't a good one, I get stubborn. It's really not a great character trait to have—especially when it comes to my relationship with God.

Commit your actions to the Lord, and your plans will succeed (Proverbs 16:3).

- What do you think it means to "commit your actions to the Lord?" What's another way that YOU might say that?
- Is it easy or hard for you to "commit your actions to God?"
- What's one area where it's easy?
- What's one area where it's hard?

For me, I usually know—somewhere deep inside—that God knows best. But I don't always like asking for God's advice because I don't want to give up my way of doing things. Usually this is because I feel like I'll be happier doing things my way.

- What's one area of your life where doing things God's way seems to be less fun than doing it your way?
- Look back at today's verse. What does it say will happen if we commit our actions to God?

According to this verse, if we give our actions to God, our plans will succeed. Or to put it another way, "we'll find the REAL life that we were made for."

- Can you see a way in which doing things God's way in the long run would work out better?

At first, doing things your own way may seem better or be more fun than doing things God's way. But sooner or later, God's way always proves to be the best way.

Hanging out with God
Spend some time praying to God today. If you know there's an area of your life where you're not trusting that God's way is best, spend time talking to him about that.

This space is here for you to jot down some thoughts, write out a prayer, draw a picture, or do whatever you want to help you remember your 10-minute moment.

Day 14

HELPING THE HELPLESS

Every school has a kid that—seemingly—is the least popular kid in the entire world. He's the one everybody makes fun of—even the unpopular kids pick on him. When I was in junior high his name was Andrew.

Now granted, Andrew was a little weird. He was poor and couldn't afford to dress like everybody else. He had really big, blonde curly hair. When I say "big" hair, I mean BIG hair—like 2 feet tall! In addition to his hair issues, Andrew constantly interrupted people, he bragged about stuff everybody knew wasn't true, and he always acted up in class to draw attention to himself. The result: Andrew was one of the loneliest, least liked kids in school, and everybody picked on him. He was so helpless that when we were in eighth grade, sixth-grade girls would tease him!

I suppose it's easy to pick on those who are different and don't fit in, but God doesn't like it—at all!

Those who mock the poor insult their Maker; those who rejoice at the misfortune of others will be punished (Proverbs 17:5).

- What does God say we are doing when we make fun of people?
- Why do you think God takes this so seriously?

- There are different ways to be "poor" than just not having money. What are some other things that people can have less of than others?
- Can you think of someone in your life that is picked on all the time? Why do people make fun of this person?
- How do you think God sees this person?
- What is one thing you could do this week to make this person's life easier or show them God's love?

Hang out with God

One of the big themes of the Bible is that God expects his people to help the helpless—people less fortunate. Today, pray for the people in your life that need help. Ask God to give you ideas on how to help them and to give you the courage to do it.

This space is here for you to jot down some thoughts, write out a prayer, draw a picture, or do whatever you want to help you remember your 10-minute moment.

Day 15

FRIEND ME

I am always amazed by people who are super selfless in their relationships. I know some people who seem to constantly look for ways to make their friends' lives a little better. I, on the other hand, tend to constantly look for ways my friends can make MY life a little better. It's not that I don't WANT to be a good friend—I just tend to be so busy that I overlook people.

Now, sometimes this is just a small problem, but every once in a while I miss something huge. Someone will need to talk—and I'm too busy to listen. Someone is clearly upset—but I'm too self-centered to ask what's wrong. And then I'll find out later that my friend REALLY needed some help.

2 MINUTES

A friend is always loyal, and a brother is born to help in time of need (Proverbs 17:17).

5 MINUTES

- Who are some of your really close friends? List their names below, and then put one word next to them that describes what you like about them.

- When you think about your friends, do you think you do as good a job looking out for their needs as they do looking out for yours?
- According to this verse "a brother is born to help in time of need." What's another way of saying that?
- Can you think of a friend in your life who is going through a hard time with something? How can you help that person?

Hanging out with God
One of the most loving things we can do for our friends is pray for them. Try to imagine what some of your friends may need, and spend some time praying to God about this stuff. While you're doing this, remember that God loves these people even more than you do!

This space is here for you to jot down some thoughts, write out a prayer, draw a picture, or do whatever you want to help you remember your 10-minute moment.

Day 16

CHEER UP

I have a friend who is an all-around good guy. He's loyal. He tries to be kind to people. He's really wise. There's just one problem: He is always seeing the negative side of things. The fancy term for this is that he's a "pessimist." No matter what happens, my friend always seems to have an attitude that says, "Yeah that was great, but it'll probably just end up bad."

Although my friend's great, after awhile I get tired of being around him. He has an incredible gift of killing really good moods.

2 MINUTES

A cheerful heart is good medicine, but a broken spirit saps a person's strength (Proverbs 17:22).

5 MINUTES

- How is someone having a cheerful heart like "good medicine?" What do you think that means?
- What do you think the term "a broken spirit" means?
- Can you think of anyone who seems to have a broken spirit?
- Generally, do you tend to focus on the things that are going well or the things that aren't going well?
- Do you tend to see the good in others or focus on their problems?

- Do you give up easily, or do you tend to push through difficult tasks?
- Why do you think being a pessimist—focusing on the negative all the time—IS NOT a Christ-like trait to have?

Hanging out with God
God's plan for all of us is to know that because he's in charge and loves us, we have reason to hope. We shouldn't always be negative! Below, write a list of three things that you're worried/stressed/feeling negative about. Briefly pray for each of them. Then make a list of three things that you are happy to have in your life. Thank God for each of them.

This space is here for you to jot down some thoughts, write out a prayer, draw a picture, or do whatever you want to help you remember your 10-minute moment.

Day 17   FIGHT

I have a strange habit of finding myself in the middle of arguments—
not serious arguments about anything important, but silly little
arguments about silly little things. This is probably because I tend to
have an opinion about EVERYTHING. A conversation about music
can quickly turn into a debate over who is the greatest band of all
time, what boy band has the best hair, and so on. When I was in
junior high I got into a pretty heated "discussion" with my buddies
about which team in the American League West was the best (for
your information it was and is and will always be the Angels). I'm not
proud to admit this, but I have hurt a few friendships over the years
with my insistence on always being right. Apparently they couldn't
handle the fact that I'm always right!

Maybe you know a friend like this—someone who turns
EVERYTHING into a disagreement. Maybe you are that person
sometimes. Whatever the case, this isn't how God wants us to be.

An offended friend is harder to win back than a fortified city.
Arguments separate friends like a gate locked with bars
(Proverbs 18:19).

- According to this verse, what do arguments do?
- Have you ever had an argument that ended up ruining a
  friendship? What was the argument over?

- If you had it to do over again, would you do something differently?
- If someone asked your friends, would they say you're easy or hard to get along with?

For me, I'm constantly sharing my opinions for one of two reasons:
1. because I'm not thinking about the feelings of others or
2. because I'm feeling a little insecure and think I need to prove that I'm smart.

Whatever YOUR reason, God's plan for your life is to develop GREAT friendships—and that means avoiding unnecessary arguments.

Hanging out with God
Spend some time today praying for the friends in your life. Ask God to show you how you can be kind/aware of what they need today. Also, if there is a friendship in your life that has been messed up by an argument, ask God to help you know how you can heal that.

This space is here for you to jot down some thoughts, write out a prayer, draw a picture, or do whatever you want to help you remember your 10-minute moment.

Day 18

HOW TO BE ATTRACTIVE

Let me ask you a question: How attractive are you? Even though that seems like an odd question coming from somebody as old as your dad, it is probably a question you have asked yourself a few times. You see, we live in a culture that is obsessed with looks. It seems like the pretty people have the best lives while short, bald people in their 40s like me get left behind (cue sad music here). But what if I were to tell you that attractiveness really has more to do with what you have happening on the inside than what you have happening on the outside? Is it possible to be attractive even though you aren't the cutest kid in your school? Is it possible that the cutest kid at school really isn't all that attractive after all?

2 MINUTES

Loyalty makes a person attractive. It is better to be poor than dishonest (Proverbs 19:22).

5 MINUTES

- The Bible says that loyalty makes a person attractive. What do you think that means? Is it true?
- What are some other internal characteristics that you think might make someone attractive?
- The verse also says it's better to be poor than dishonest. That sounds good, but do you really believe it's true?
- Have you ever been dishonest to avoid an awkward situation?
- Do you consider yourself to be a fairly loyal friend? What would your friends say about you?

- Would you say you're pretty honest with your friends, or do you keep things from them?

The truth is that a lot of us obsess about being outwardly attractive—wearing the right clothes, catching the opposite sex's attention, getting ourselves in shape—but God says that the most IMPORTANT thing is to work on our inward attractiveness. That's the stuff that will really last.

Hanging out with God
Spend some time praying today about becoming a more inwardly attractive person. Ask God to show you how you can be loyal and honest to the people around you.

This space is here for you to jot down some thoughts, write out a prayer, draw a picture, or do whatever you want to help you remember your 10-minute moment.

Day 19

BEING DRUNK ≠ BEING SMART

If it hasn't happened to you already, it will soon: You'll be at a party, or at a friend's house, or somewhere else, and someone will offer you alcohol.

Now the Christian answer to this is easy: The law says people your age aren't supposed to drink, so you shouldn't drink. But the truth is that knowing the right answer doesn't always mean doing the right thing. Every Christian must examine this issue, and it's important for you—at this time in your life—to decide what you believe about alcohol.

Wine produces mockers; alcohol leads to brawls. Those led astray by drink cannot be wise (Proverbs 20:1).

- List all of the things that this verse says alcohol leads to.
- In what ways do you think this is true?
- If you have friends who drink—or if you do sometimes—have you ever seen any of the behavior this verse describes?
- Why do you think people choose to get drunk?

I want to be clear about something at this point—the Bible doesn't say that it's wrong for adults to drink alcohol. As a matter of fact, there's a story where Jesus changes water to wine at a wedding!

But the Bible does pretty consistently say that getting drunk shouldn't be a characteristic of someone who follows Jesus.

- Why do you think that is? What is it about being drunk that isn't consistent with being a Christian?

The truth is pretty obvious: When we get drunk we don't make very good decisions. As a matter of fact, some people (and unfortunately this is especially true with teenagers) tend to make really, really damaging decisions when they're drunk: They drive when they know they shouldn't, they try things they otherwise wouldn't, or they treat people poorly. I think everyone can pretty much agree—being drunk doesn't lead to making great decisions!

And this, I think, is God's big problem with it. The whole point of Proverbs is that God wants us to be people who make wise choices, who think things through. It's really hard to do that when getting drunk. Now someday, when you turn 21, you'll have to decide for yourself what type of role you want alcohol to play in your life, but I want to challenge you to not drink while you're underage. And the other challenge is that if you ever do decide to drink that you would follow God's wisdom and not let it influence your life and actions in a way you might regret.

3 MINUTES

Hanging out with God
Some of you may be thinking, "I'd NEVER do that." Some of you are thinking, "I've ALREADY done that." And some of you are thinking, "I don't know what I feel about this." Wherever you are on this topic, spend some time praying to God about this area of your life. Ask God to give you the wisdom and the strength to make wise choices concerning alcohol.

THOUGHTS

This space is here for you to jot down some thoughts, write out a prayer, draw a picture, or do whatever you want to help you remember your 10-minute moment.

Day 20

WHY GETTING
EVEN
NEVER WORKS

I have to admit—some of my favorite movies are the ones where the bad guy gets caught in the end. It's even better if the person they wronged gets some sort of sweet revenge! I think that happened in The Brave Little Toaster—umm, maybe not. But for my money the best movies are the ones that end really badly for the really bad guys.

But for lots of people, revenge is more than just something that happens in movies. Lots of people believe getting revenge is the best way to "get back" at somebody who has wronged them. Maybe it's a teacher, or a friend, or an enemy, or a random person who wronged us in some way. But here's the problem—getting even with somebody never really gets things right.

2 MINUTES

Don't say, "I will get even for this wrong." Wait for the Lord to handle the matter (Proverbs 20:22).

5 MINUTES

- Has someone ever done something to you that made you want to get even?
- What did this person do?
- How did that make you feel?
- Why do we think getting even will help? What are we hoping to get out of it?

- According to this verse, what should we do when we want to get even?
- Be completely honest: How does this advice make you feel?

I'm not going to lie—the idea of waiting for God to "handle the matter" doesn't seem very satisfying to me. But throughout the Bible we're told the same thing: Don't get even; let God handle it. I think there are two reasons for this. 1) Just because we think we know what's fair doesn't mean we do. Often people get revenge and end up doing something even worse than the first person. And honestly, if you "get even," doesn't that kind of make you like the person you're mad at? 2) We forgive others because God has forgiven us.

Seriously, have you ever thought about how much God forgives us? I mean, he's GOD! But God always let's us come back to him, even when we ignore or disobey him for days, or weeks, or months! God says that when we understand how much we've been forgiven, it's easier for us to forgive others.

Hanging out with God
Is there someone in your life that you want to get even with? Pray that God would—over time—help you forgive this person. Ask God to keep you from becoming someone who is always bitter or angry at people who have wronged you. If you're really bold, ask God to give you opportunities to do something nice for this person.

THOUGHTS

This space is here for you to jot down some thoughts, write out a prayer, draw a picture, or do whatever you want to help you remember your 10-minute moment.

Day 21

THE SHAM BEHIND
THE 'WOW'!

There's one reason—and one reason only—why infomercials exist: because there are people like me in the world. I don't like admitting it, but I'm an impulse buyer. I see something I THINK I need (like a juicer, or a knife that could cut through my shoes, or—wait for it—the "Sham-Wow!").

But have you ever stopped to think about what commercials are really trying to do? Next time you're watching TV pay close attention during the commercials and you'll notice that each one is saying something like this: "Right now you're life kind of stinks, BUT, if you buy our BRAND-NEW product, then you'll be happy for the rest of your life!"

OK, I'm exaggerating a little, but you get the idea. We live in a world that's constantly saying "you need more!" But according to the Bible, this kind of thinking leads to nothing but trouble.

2 MINUTES

Those who love pleasure become poor; those who love wine and luxury will never be rich (Proverbs 21:17).

5 MINUTES

- What do you think it means to "love pleasure?" How would you describe that in your own words?
- Why do you think the Bible says people who love pleasure become poor? Do you think that's true? Why or why not?

There's an obvious side to this verse: If I'm always buying knives off of TV, I'll eventually run out of money. But there's something else going on in this verse, too—its warning against becoming the kind of people who always need the next new thing.

- Are you usually happy with the stuff you have, or do you always seem to want more?
- Do you tend to be jealous of what other people have?
- What is it about new stuff (clothes, video games, phones) that makes us want it so much?
- The Bible talks elsewhere about always being content. How does always wanting new stuff get in the way of that?

Hanging out with God

Truth is, there's always something in life we're not content about. What is one thing in your life right now that you wish was different? Spend some time talking to God about that today. As you're praying, ask God to help you be content with what you have right now.

This space is here for you to jot down some thoughts, write out a prayer, draw a picture, or do whatever you want to help you remember your 10-minute moment.

Day 22

THE KID FROM THE DOMINICAN REPUBLIC

I'm not sure if other people are like this or not, but it can be really hard for me to grasp that God loves every other person in the world—all 6 billion of them—just as much as he loves me. I KNOW it's true, but I think my world tends to be so self-focused—I'm always thinking about MY day, MY needs, MY wants, MY plans—that sometimes I slip into thinking that God is probably only thinking about my stuff too. So when I pray to God, I spend a lot of the time praying about ME.

But then I see a picture of someone from another country—like the one I saw recently of a impoverished, sick kid from the Dominican Republic—and it hits me: God cares just as much about this kid's needs as he does about mine.

2 MINUTES

The rich and poor have this in common: The Lord made them both (Proverbs 22:2).

5 MINUTES

- Why do you think this verse was put in the Bible? Why is it an important thing to know?
- Is it easy or hard for you to think about the needs of other people? Do you spend a lot of time thinking about others, or not?
- If it's hard for you (it isn't for some people!), why is it so hard? What gets in the way?

I think my problem is this: If God cares about that kid in the Dominican Republic as much as he does about me, then my view of the world is all messed up. If God cares about that kid in the Dominican Republic, then I probably should, too.

- What are some of the needs in the world that you can think of? Take a minute to list a few.
- What are some of the resources God has given you? What stuff do you have that most people in the world don't?
- Can you think of two or three things you could do over the next few weeks to help meet the needs of other, less fortunate people?
- What are some of the needs of people you see every day? List a few (they don't have to be about money).
- What are some of the ways you can help meet these people's needs?

The big idea is this: God loves other people just as much as he loves us, and when we get that, it inspires us to care for them, too.

Hanging out with God
Spend some time today praying for the poor/hungry/sick people in the world. Ask God to show you ways you can begin helping meet those needs. Also, pray for people around you that you know need help. Ask God to show you opportunities to help them too.

THOUGHTS

This space is here for you to jot down some thoughts, write out a prayer, draw a picture, or do whatever you want to help you remember your 10-minute moment.

Day 23

BUT **THEY** GET TO

Let's be honest: Following God's way of living is sometimes REALLY hard. I mean, God says not to gossip about others, but sometimes not talking bad about someone who hurt us is SO difficult. God says to not lust in our hearts and to stay sexually pure, but sometimes it seems like our bodies are just going out of control! God says to consider others first, instead of always doing what's best for us. But most days that seems almost impossible.

But you know what makes it even harder? That many (maybe most!) of our friends are getting to do whatever they want. While we're trying not to gossip, they're talking behind one another's backs all day long. While we're trying to stay sexually pure, they're looking at all kinds of stuff or talking about things we know we're supposed to avoid. While we're trying to be considerate of others, some of our friends seem to be treating people poorly and having fun while doing it! Honestly, sometimes it's hard not be a little—well, jealous.

2 MINUTES

Don't envy sinners, but always continue to fear the Lord. You will be rewarded for this; your hope will not be disappointed (Proverbs 23:17-18).

49

- Being really honest, what's one of the hardest areas of your life to obey God right now? What makes it so tough?
- Are people around you helping you be the person God wants you to be in that area, or not?

- Have you ever wished God would change his mind about what he expects from us?
- Even though disobeying God—sinning—may look good, do you really think it's a better way to live?
- What does the second half of this verse say will happen for those who obey God?

Now, I'd like to be able to promise you that if you obey God, everything will always work out really well, and it will be super easy, and you'll see right away that God's way really IS best. But you want to know the truth? It usually doesn't work like that.

But I think what this verse means is this: If you choose to keep learning how to obey God, and to let him be in charge of your life, he will turn you into the kind of person that you would REALLY want to be. Because let's be honest: No one wants to be someone who always talks bad about others, or who is consumed by lust, or who is super selfish. When God says "you will be rewarded" I think this at least PART of what this means. God will reward us by making us who we really want to be.

3 MINUTES

Hanging out with God
Today, ask God to help you realize that sin is never the right choice. Ask him to help you see why even though some of that stuff might look good, it really leads you down a path you don't want to travel.

THOUGHTS

This space is here for you to jot down some thoughts, write out a prayer, draw a picture, or do whatever you want to help you remember your 10-minute moment.

Day 24

BE HONEST WITH ME

I like to think of myself as a pretty honest guy. I don't cheat, I try not to lie, and if somebody asks me a question, I do my best to offer an honest answer. Most of the time, being honest comes easily for me. I said MOST of the time! When I find it tough to be honest is when a friend or somebody I care about needs me to be honest, but I know my honesty will be tough for that person to handle. If I see a friend doing something I know they shouldn't, I find it hard to be honest about the behavior because I don't want to cause a strain in our friendship. When an eighth-grade boy in my small group asks me if he looks good in skinny jeans, I usually say "yes" even though I really think they make him look more like a fifth-grade girl!

But according to today's verse, when I do that I'm not acting like a true friend.

An honest answer is like a kiss of friendship (Proverbs 24:26).

- Have you ever had a moment—maybe like one of the ones I described above—when telling the truth would make things awkward? What did you do?
- Why is telling the truth to a friend hard sometimes?
- Do you think we avoid these conversations to protect our friends or to protect ourselves?

52

- What are some ways that NOT telling a friend the truth is actually selfish?
- Is there an area in your life right now where you've lied to someone close to you? What can you do to make that right?

I suppose if there's a main point to today's verse it's this: Real friends tell the truth. Even when it's hard. Even when it makes us look bad. Even when it's something our friend doesn't want to hear. But one of the key things to remember is this: Real friends tell the truth IN LOVE. We tell our friends the truth with humility, knowing that someday soon our friend will probably need to show this same tough love to us.

- What are some of the differences between telling someone the truth and telling that person the truth in love? Describe some characteristics that make the second option different.

Hanging out with God
Spend some time today praying for a friend that you need to give "an honest answer" to, whether that's calling them out on something they've done/are doing or coming clean about a lie that you told. Ask God to help the conversation go well, and that this conversation would make the friendship stronger.

This space is here for you to jot down some thoughts, write out a prayer, draw a picture, or do whatever you want to help you remember your 10-minute moment.

Day 25

DON'T BE A
FLAKE

Do you know what a "flake" is? I'm not talking about a corn flake or a snow flake or a flake of dandruff. The "flake" I'm talking about is the person who seems to have a habit of promising to be somewhere or do something but not following through—this person "flakes" out. Today's verse doesn't actually use the word "flake," but it could.

2 MINUTES

A person who promises a gift but doesn't give it is like clouds and wind that bring no rain (Proverbs 25:14).

5 MINUTES

- Can you think of a time when a friend didn't come through for you? How did that make you feel?
- This verse says a flaky friend is like "clouds and wind that bring no rain." What do you think that means?
- Would your friends describe you as someone who follows through on what you say? If not, why not?

3 MINUTES

Hanging out with God
Spend some time today taking an honest look at yourself. How "flaky" are you? Are you somebody people can count on?

In your prayer time today, ask God to help you work on the "flaky" areas of your life. If there is somebody you have let down recently, ask God to give you the courage to go to that person and apologize.

This space is here for you to jot down some thoughts, write out a prayer, draw a picture, or do whatever you want to help you remember your 10-minute moment.

Day 26

FRIENDS SHOULD BE LIKE KNIFE SHARPENERS

When I was in high school, I had two groups of friends. One group was made up of kids from my youth group who loved Jesus and tried to live their lives his way. They challenged me spiritually, called me out when I messed up, and genuinely wanted the best for me. The other group was the exact opposite. None of them went to church, none of them gave a rip about Jesus, and they certainly didn't care if I was living up to my potential. The truth is that one of my groups of friends sharpened me and made me a better person and the other group only served to "dull" me.

2 MINUTES

As iron sharpens iron, so a friend sharpens a friend (Proverbs 27:17).

5 MINUTES

- Back in the day, people used to sharpen swords or tools with another iron object. If you've ever seen someone use a flint rock to sharpen a knife, it was kind of like that. How can friendships also be like that?
- What are some ways that friends "sharpen" each other?
- Think through your friendships. What are some ways your friends "sharpen" you? How do you "sharpen" them?
- Sometimes friendships don't sharpen us spiritually but instead dull us (make us feel farther away from God). Do you think your friendships SHARPEN you spiritually or make you DULLER?

- What is one friendship in your life that God could use to make you both spiritually sharper?

Hanging out with God

You will probably always have some friends who "dull" you, which is why you need to make sure you also have plenty of friends who are like knife sharpeners—friends who make you sharper when you are around them. Today, spend some time in prayer asking God to help you become the type of friend that sharpens others and to bring friends into your life who can do the same thing for you.

This space is here for you to jot down some thoughts, write out a prayer, draw a picture, or do whatever you want to help you remember your 10-minute moment.

Day 27

KURT THE COWARDLY LION... OR NOT

I don't know why, but I've never been a big fan of the movie *The Wizard of Oz*. I think it has something to do with those creepy flying monkeys. But there is one character I like: the Cowardly Lion. I mean, here is this lion, who is supposed to be the most powerful animal around, but in *The Wizard of Oz*, he is anything but powerful—he is a total coward.

Sometimes I feel a little like the Cowardly Lion. I spend my days afraid that people aren't going to like me because of something I said. Or I'm afraid I won't be able to get everything done. Sometimes I'm afraid to talk to people about God because they'll think I'm weird. Or I'm afraid to obey God because I think his way will end up backfiring on me.

But the good news is, God has something better than this for me—and for you, too! Today's verse reminds us that not all lions are cowards.

The wicked run away when no one is chasing them, but the godly are bold as lions (Proverbs 28:1).

- In your own words, what does this verse say is the difference between godly people and wicked people?

- Why do you think godly people aren't afraid? What do they understand that other people don't?
- Romans 8:31 says, "If God is for us, who can ever be against us?" Rewrite that verse in your own words.

- What is one area where you are fearful, like the Cowardly Lion? What is it about that thing that scares you?
- If God were to talk to you right now about that scary thing, what do you think he'd say?

The truth is that God wants us to be bold lions, not cowardly ones. It says in the Bible that the same power that raised Jesus from the grave is at work inside of us (Romans 8:11). If that's true, then we don't have to fear ANYTHING!

Hanging out with God
Spend some time talking to God about the thing that scares you. Ask God to give you confidence and courage when you face that thing this week. Remember in the moment of fear this week to ask God to help you.

This space is here for you to jot down some thoughts, write out a prayer, draw a picture, or do whatever you want to help you remember your 10-minute moment.

Day 28

COME OUT, COME OUT, WHEREVER YOU ARE!

Do you remember playing hide-and-seek as a kid? You'd find the perfect hiding spot, tucked away and out of sight where no one could ever find you, and then you'd freeze in that spot and try not to move a muscle. For the good hiders, this would go on for a very long time. For the REALLY good hiders who were never found, there came a point when someone would shout "come out, come out, wherever you are!" and then everyone would know that it was safe to come out now.

Sometimes we live like this in our everyday lives. We have stuff going on that we don't want anyone to know about—so we hide. We disobey our parents—and we hide. We are failing behind in our classes—and we hide. We have some stuff in our life that we know is harmful for us—maybe even illegal—and we're desperately hiding that stuff from our parents, teachers, and youth workers at church. Just about everyone is hiding in some way. And some of us have gotten really good at it.

2 MINUTES

People who conceal their sins will not prosper, but if they confess and turn from them, they will receive mercy (Proverbs 28:13).

5 MINUTES

- What do you think the word "prosper" means? What's another way of saying the first half of this verse?
- Can you remember a time when you tried to hide something you did wrong? How did that story end?
- This verse talks about confessing sins. What do you think it means to "confess"?
- Who do you think we should confess to?

Here's the truth: When we do something wrong we hide because we're afraid of the consequences. Or maybe it's because we're ashamed of what we've done. Whatever the case, God says that if we hide our sins they will just continue to hurt us. BUT if we confess our sins—first to God, and then to the person we're hiding from—that we'll receive mercy, which is kind of like saying we'll be forgiven. God is basically saying, "come out, come out, wherever you are!" It's safe to come out now. You can stop hiding.

3 MINUTES

Hanging out with God
Spend some time talking to God about the things in your life you are hiding from him. Remember when talking to God that he already knows and has forgiven you—he just wants you to accept his forgiveness.

Also, if there is someone in your life you need to make things right with, pray that God would give you the strength to know how to do that.

THOUGHTS

This space is here for you to jot down some thoughts, write out a prayer, draw a picture, or do whatever you want to help you remember your 10-minute moment.

Day 29

ASK ME ANYTHING

One of my favorite scenes from the movie *Aladdin* is where the Genie is explaining to Aladdin that he can ask for ANYTHING (well, almost anything) he wants. Anything he wants... Awesome!

Now imagine that you're having a similar conversation with God, and he's telling you the same thing: You can ask for whatever you want. What would it be? Seriously—go ahead and think about your answer.

In today's verse the writer of this proverb—a guy named Agur—tells God he wants just two things before he dies—but the things he asks for are really weird!

2 MINUTES

O God, I beg two favors from you; let me have them before I die. First, help me never to tell a lie. Second, give me neither poverty nor riches! Give me just enough to satisfy my needs. For if I grow rich, I may deny you and say, "Who is the Lord?" And if I am too poor, I may steal and thus insult God's holy name (Proverbs 30:7-9).

5 MINUTES

- What are the two things Agur asks for?
- Agur's second request is kind of weird. Why does he not want to be poor? Why doesn't he want to be rich?
- For Agur, what do being poor and being rich both have in common? How do both affect his relationship with God?

Here's what I think is cool about this verse: Agur is basically saying, "God, I don't want ANYTHING to be a distraction from me obeying and following and knowing you." Agur looks at the world around him and sees that people who are rich think they don't need God. But he sees people who are poor and observes that they are tempted to do things not honoring to God just to survive. So he prays that God would eliminate any temptation not to focus on him.

- Agur was SUPER interested in God being the center of his life—but he also knew that wasn't easy. What about for you? Why do you think it can be hard to keep God at the center of our lives? What are some of the distractions in your life that keep you from giving time to God?
- What is one thing you could give up for a week, and instead use that time to focus on God?

Hanging out with God

During your prayer time today, offer the one thing you're going to give up for the week to God. Tell him that you don't want anything to get in the way of your relationship. Ask God to speak to you this week as you try to spend more time with him.

Also, it might be a good idea to tell someone about what you're giving up this week, just so you have a little accountability. Who are some people that can help you stick with this commitment?

THOUGHTS

This space is here for you to jot down some thoughts, write out a prayer, draw a picture, or do whatever you want to help you remember your 10-minute moment.

Day 30

THE GOOD GIRL

There are a lot—A LOT!—of messages in the world today about what women should be like, and most of these messages are pretty shallow.

Now, there are always exceptions, but most women are famous because of how stunningly, unrealistically beautiful they are. The next time you're in a grocery store, pay attention to the magazines that are in the checkout line. They're all saying one thing: "Girls that guys would desire must look like this."

But what is really, really awful about this is the pressure it puts on girls—especially younger teenage girls. Maybe some of you reading this right now know just what I'm talking about. Every day you feel the pressure to be taller, thinner, better dressed, more flirtatious, more desirable.

And guys, we aren't immune to this. We also see this stuff, and we start becoming OBSESSED with looks. We start thinking of girls only as objects that exist for us to look at.

But the Bible says that what REALLY makes a girl valuable ISN'T what she looks like…

Charm is deceptive, and beauty does not last; but a woman who fears the Lord will be greatly praised. Reward her for all she has done. Let her deeds publicly declare her praise (Proverbs 31:30-31).

- Have you ever seen a before/after picture of someone who used to be a beautiful girl in Hollywood? If so, you know that beauty doesn't last. What does this verse say DOES last?
- This verse says that "charm" is deceptive. What's another word here for charm? Why is it deceptive?
- For the girls: Do you feel pressure to look a certain way? If so, why do you think that's so important to you?
- For the girls: If you were to be really honest, what do you want a guy to find most desirable about you: how you look or who you really are?
- For the girls: Do you tend to focus on guys who notice how you look or who you are?
- For the girls: How do you think God sees you?
- For the girls: What does that last sentence say a girl should be known for? If your looks were determined only by your actions, would people think you're beautiful?
- For the guys: With girls, have you ever been interested in someone who was very pretty, but you knew wasn't a girl you should be with? Why were her looks so important?
- For the guys: Have you ever thought about what kind of character you'd look for in a girl? What are some of the qualities that would be important to you?
- For the guys: Do you tend to only pay attention to pretty girls? If so, what message do you think your actions are sending to girls in general about what you think is most important? How do your actions toward girls make them feel?

Here's the truth: 60 years from now, none of us are going to be very attractive. (When's the last time you saw someone in their 70s you thought was hot?) Ultimately, what matters most is what kind of person we are internally. Outwardly we're getting a little bit older every day, but internally, if we're moving toward God in our life, we're becoming a little more beautiful.

3 MINUTES

Hanging out with God
Girls: Spend some time today talking to God about whatever thoughts/feelings/hurts this devotion brought up. Ask God to help you see yourself the way HE sees you. If you struggle with this, ask God to free you from needing guys' attention to feel special.

Guys: Spend some time today asking God to help you see girls the way HE sees them. If you're struggling with lust, ask God to help you with that (it might also be a good idea to invite someone to help keep you accountable with that issue—I know that's tough, but it's super important).

THOUGHTS

This space is here for you to jot down some thoughts, write out a prayer, draw a picture, or do whatever you want to help you remember your 10-minute moment.